How to be an Objection Master

By

Jason Morris

Real Estate Agents that REALLY work

Introduction (Please Read)

I have been selling real estate for 15+ years. If you feel like any of the objection handling strategies I am going to give you are "borderline" or "whatever term you want to insert here"... Don't use them. These are ideas and ways that I have personally handled objections in the past.

When in doubt, hang up, follow up in a few days. There is a good chance they won't even remember who you are.

This book is meant to give you examples of ways I have personally handled seller objections in the past and give you ideas on how you can handle seller objections in the future.

I also included some initial ideas and beliefs I have when it comes to the real estate industry. I want you to understand my point of view when it comes to handling objections and making calls.

You can also check out my other books on Amazon:
How to be an Expired Master
How to be a FSBO Master
Follow up Master Day Planner

Table of contents

For more information or to join my group coaching you can go to
http://www.JasonMorrisGroupCoaching.com 4

What is an objection?

The Oxford Dictionary describes an objection as:

ob·jec·tion

/əbˈjekSH(ə)n/

noun

1. an expression or feeling of disapproval or opposition; a reason for disagreeing

What I believe it is:

I believe an objection is really just an excuse not to do something now. In the case of this book, it is a real estate property seller telling you their "go-to" line that is often just something to get you off the phone.

The "sales objection" is a direct response in the evolution to our ancestors physiological reaction of flight or fight that occurs in the presence of something terrifying, either mentally or physically.

In modern society we are not experiencing this reaction due to attacking wild animals, it is the response to the common sales call.

Its a smoke screen, nothing more. For most agents it is a minor tactic that defeats them and somehow gets them to give up on their goals.

Most agents create more objections than they will ever overcome because they refuse to learn scripts, stick to them and practice.

My real estate business beliefs

I need to tell you on these first pages what my real estate business beliefs and ideas are. All of this information comes from my 15+ years in the real estate business and from coaching thousands of agents all over North America. You can get more information on my coaching program at www.JasonMorrisGroupCoaching.com

1. I believe we are not in the business of selling houses. We sell a service that sells houses.

   I believe this service needs to have the ability to be replicated over and over. Just like McDonalds, they are not changing the temperature of your hamburger because you prefer it medium well. They are willing to add ketchup and mustard, but the actual cheeseburger, the bun and the process never actually changes.

   I believe that our business needs to be a sales system that is designed to market the homes that fit in what you have identified as your ideal client or the people you want to work with. If their home does no't fit, you probably should not be their agent.

2. We need to have a written marketing plan. In this book, I will call it a pre-listing package, a marketing plan or information about myself, my team and what we do to sell houses.

   Most agents do not have anything in writing they could send a seller client right now if they needed to. The ones that do have something, rarely send it. It sits on their laptop in a secret folder because, heaven forbid another agent get a glimpse of it.

   Every other profession has marketing material that tells about their service. We should have the same. You can download my free template at www.JasonMorrisPrelistingPackage.com

3. The purpose of prospecting on the phone for sellers is to set appointments and meet sellers face to face, not to list the house. I often see agents struggle with this and try to pressure the seller over the phone to commit to the listing. This is extremely hard to do. It is kind of like a guy asking a girl to marry them before they have been on the first date.

   I believe that we should set up the listing appointment and then let our sales process actually do the work of listing the home.

4. Follow up is really the key to massive real estate sales success. If you do not have a follow up plan you will fail. You can get a full 1 year follow

up plan at www.FollowupMasterDayPlanner.com

5. If you set up your business so you can replicate your high income producing daily activities, you can build a predictable business with predictable income.

These ideas are the basis for my real estate group coaching program. To help agents build a business that actually works for them. One with a schedule and predictable income. Not the roller coaster most agents are riding.

With these things in mind, many of the objection handling strategies will make more sense and become more usable in your business.

If you want to join my group coaching, you can get more information at www.JasonMorrisGroupcoaching.com

Biggest Problem Most Agents have

The biggest problem most real estate agent are having, overcoming objections or just sales calls in general, is they think there is a magic bullet.YThey think there is a phrase or some sort of (insert the latest BS piece of technology) that is going to work 100% of the time.

Nothing works 100% of the time. If we really want to get honest about conversion numbers, the odds of you making 1 random phone call, setting an appointment, showing up and listing the house, is very small.

If that is what you are hoping for, you will starve to death.

BUT....There are so many agents that expect this and think this it is realistic.

It is not.

I blame Hollywood. Everyone has watched movies like *Boiler Room*, *Jerry Mcguire* and *The Wolf of Wall Street*.

All of these movies contain, what I would call, "Asshole Sales Objection Scripts" or in short "A SOS". Which is exactly what it is.

Wikipedia defines "SOS" as morse code for a distress signal. The sales people using these scripts are in distress mode. I have heard it called "commission breath". Typically, it is just desperation. They will do or say anything they think will lead them to a commission check.

These 'A SOS" scripts are where you tell your buyer/seller something that is just completely out of left field that really is just offensive or belittling.

One of the best sales scenes in The Wolf of Wall Street, is an example of this. You see Leonardo DiCaprio (Jordan Belfort) has a guy on speaker phone and everyone is crowded around him. This guy clearly does not want to buy the stock he is being pitched.

All of a sudden the character, Jordan Belfort, delivers a well rehearsed line that is really just offensive and this guy on the phone goes from a complete non-believer to a believer and buys.

There is only 1 place, I know, that "A SOS" scripts work well and that is Hollywood.

There is one thing you have to accept when prospecting sellers, I like to use this professional baseball analogy:

No one in baseball bats 1.000.
If you got on base 4 out of 10 at bats consistently, you will be a Hall of Fame player.
If you got on base just 3 out of 10 times consistently, you would be paid A REAL LOT OF MONEY

We are working in an industry where if you listed 3 out of 10 properties you went on listing appointments for and went on appointments consistently every week, you will take a boat load of property listings and **make a lot of money**.

However, our industry has one unique advantage over playing baseball. If you strike out or you blow the listing appointment or you just are really bad at the whole process, you can still follow up and have a 2nd chance at listing that seller's property. You can get a "do over" and can go back to bat again. It is not unrealistic to get really good on the phone, build a great followup plan and list 70 to 80%+ of the listing appointments you go on!

I wrote this book based on objections I have received and objections that were crowd sourced from my group coaching and my Facebook group Real Estate Agents that REALLY work.

This is a book of scripts and strategies to overcome objections. These are not "A SOS" scripts, they are real life strategies and scripts.

I hope you enjoy what I have put together and I hope it makes you a ton of money!

How many objections have you given today?

I defined what an objection was at the beginning of this book.

We are a society that we are continuously being sold to. All of us have our "go to" objections we use when we are confronted with these sales pitches.

Here are some examples.

1. The gas station clerk asks you if you would like to buy a candy bar with your drink purchase.
2. The department store cashier asks you to sign up for a store credit card.
3. The Insurance person cold calling you to sell you health insurance.
4. The Real estate lead company calling you asking if you want to subscribe to their lead service.

I could keep going, but you get the point. You were probably thinking about your "go to" objection while you were reading those.

Here is the reality of those examples and your objection.

1. You don't dislike the gas station clerk. They are probably a nice person. Maybe you are on a low carb diet? Maybe you just didn't want a candy bar? Whatever your reason is, just because you didn't buy a candy bar today, does not mean you won't buy one during your next visit.

2. The department store cashier is probably a nice person. Maybe you just didn't want a new credit card? Maybe you were worried you would get turned down? Maybe you were in a hurry? But next trip to that store, there is a possibility, you could say yes.

3. The insurance salesperson cold calling people about health insurance may have the best rates and coverage in the industry. You probably won't know today, because when he called you, you had a million things going on and you just didn't have time to talk.....so… you hung up on him… maybe said "don't call back". It wasn't that you didn't need health insurance, you just didn't have time and were frustrated with other stuff.

4. The real estate lead generation company calling is something we deal with all the time. We would all love an extra deal a month, right? But they

always call at a bad time and sometimes I don't even understand what they are selling.

In each one of these examples, we used a go-to objection. These objections had nothing to do with the salesperson, the product/service or really anything. Some of the objections we give have far more personal reasons that we say no, than true disagreements with what is being offered.

Objections are a numbers game. The more people that come thru that convenience store door and are asked "would you like to add a candy bar for a dollar?". The more candy bars they will sell. Maybe it is 3 out of 10 buy? If they had 100 people come thru the store. That is 30 more candy bars sold today and an additional $900 in revenue for the month!

So the store has a conversion ratio of 3 out of 10 people buying a candy bar. I am almost certain a certain percentage of the 7 out of 10 non-buyers, think about a candy bar later and go back to the store to get one for a dollar.

Everytime you hear an objection like "Bring a buyer and I will pay you 3%", make them an offer for full representation (we cover this in more detail later in the book). You will always have a certain conversion rate, then an additional conversion rate from your follow up.

Lead sales companies follow this same model. They call us, because most of us want more leads. A certain percentage will schedule a demo. A certain percentage will buy as soon as the demo ends and then an additional percentage will buy from their sales follow up.

Generally, when sellers seems angry, short or frustrated on the phone, it is typically not you. It is often a personal situation they are in.

So why do Sellers use objections?

So why do people use objections? Why can't they just be upfront and just tell us what they are thinking? (lol) This is about as mysterious as asking your significant other "What do you want for dinner?". No one knows, but from my experience, I have a few ideas why I think sellers are giving real estate agents objections.

1. The agent does not know their scripts and they have not practiced them at all. So the phone conversation had no purpose and had no point. They got so off track during the conversation that they talked for 30 minutes about something as arbitrary as "what is your cat doing today?".

   The agent hung up the phone and never really even asked a closing question or anything about the property that was for sale. They basically just said "hey, let me list your house." then just talked randomly when the person said no.

2. The seller just isn't ready yet. This happens. Sometimes, they put a FSBO ad on craigslist and they do actually want to sell their house. But

they have no plan at all for showing the home to anyone. They have work, a spouse, kids, dog, 10 unfinished projects and they have no clue where they would go if someone showed up on their door step with a bag of cash to pay their asking price.

3. They do not have enough information about the service they are being offered or they were just misinformed about how real estate agents work.

   Imagine that, very similar reason we give lead generation companies objections. We just don't know enough about what they are doing for us.

   Believe it or not, I have been on listing appointments, where the reason why they hadn't already listed their home with an agent is, they didn't know how agents worked. I have had people that didn't know we get paid on performance. Most of us are not asking for a commission check upfront.

4. They did not know how hard it would actually be to sell their house on their own (or how costly). With only around 50% of Americans owning homes, the percentage of Americans to actually go through the experience of selling a home is pretty small. I would be willing to bet the majority

of sellers probably have never worked with an agent to sell a house or they have not sold a property in the last 5 to 7 years, in the state they are in. The number of sellers that have bought and sold multiple properties in the last 24 to 36 months are very small.

I think this is often why sellers start out very strong, "hey we are selling ourselves" is their motto. Until they realize marketing on your own is tough, buyers "stretch the truth" about finances, attorney charge a lot of money and people never want to come see your house when it is convenient. Oh and I forgot, everyone calling from craigslist is looking for a "Rent to Own" or some funky financing.

Most sellers do not understand they may have to go through hundreds of leads to find 1 person that is qualified and WANTS to buy their specific home.

5. The agent before used an "A SOS" script. The agent they talked with before was a bad agent or just rude. They only cared about making a commission check. They never answered their phone. They never had any showings or feed back. They just assume other agents will be the

same.

6. It just was not a good time. This is different than "I am not ready".Sometimes when you call a seller it just isn't a good time. Just like the examples in the last chapter. They had a million things going on, talking to a real estate agent for 5 minutes just made it a million and one things.

I am not telling you these are the only 6 reasons sellers are giving us objections, but I think this sums it all up pretty well and shows you that often an objection has very little to do with you.

On a basic level we all react a certain way to certain things. We all give objections.

Is it really an Objection? Or a Condition?

It is easy to get confused, sometimes you might not be getting the objection you think you are. Sometimes you are actually just getting a condition.

So what is a condition?

Oxford Dictionary defines it as:

con·di·tion

/kənˈdiSH(ə)n/

noun

the state of something with regard to its appearance, quality, or working order.
"the wiring is in good condition"

Often times a condition, is something that is true. The reason that seller said they can't meet you at 2pm on Tuesday is because….. They just can't meet you at 2pm on Tuesday, they have a doctors appointment or just something else going on.

It is really that simple. They have something going or happening and what you are proposing just does not work right now.

About 4 years ago, I had a seller I was talking to about selling his house. We met at the house, the husband and wife really liked me. They were moved out and the house was vacant. It looked great! But they had a couple small unfinished projects, that probably would have been a big deal for buyers getting financing, but nothing major.

A few weeks go by and we set another appointment to put the house on the market. A few days before we were going to meet, a storm blew a tree over on the roof of the house. The sellers fortunately had insurance, but it was going to take a couple weeks to get it all cleaned up and the roof repaired. They canceled on me.

A couple of weeks later we schedule another appointment to put the house on the market. The husband gets sick and gets admitted to the hospital. They canceled on me again!!

Now for most agents, they would take these cancelations as the sellers not wanting to work with them and they are just wasting their time.

I kept following up, I eventually listed their home. I sold it and made $5,000 in commissions. The people wanted to work with me, they believed in me and they were not jerking me around…. They just had something called "life" happening to them.

Difference between a Condition and an Objection

The difference is a Condition is something that is real. It is valid and often can be quantified. An Objection is often nothing more than a smoke screen. Some story they are telling you today to get you off the phone or out of their house.

What do you do when you get a condition?

You wait and you follow up. Normally the only thing that can overcome or cure a condition is time, concern and a helpful heart. Following up with the potential client because you care about their situation and you want to help them.

When you get a condition on the phone like "I can't meet tomorrow at 2pm" don't overthink it. Just ask another question such as "Will you be at work then?" let them answer and offer another time.

The Objections - 2 basic strategies

With scripts and strategies to overcome them

Let's get started.

For each of these objections, I am going to give you a simple, uncomplicated strategy to overcome that objection, some will have scripts, others will have a strategy. I don't want you to get bogged down in the details of a specific objection, My goal is for you to learn the process to overcome them.

For you all wanting to cut to the chase.

I believe that people are normally wanting to sell their house because they have a problem and they think, selling their home can fix that problem.

Strategy 1. Overcome the objection quickly and revert back to your original script.

Strategy 2. Get as much information as possible and follow up.

We are not ready to list our house

This is often nothing more than a smoke screen to get you off the phone. I would focus the conversation on "selling their house" rather than "listing" their house. After All that is what they want.

Seller: We are not ready to list our house.

Agent: no problem, you do want to sell your house, correct? (let them answer)

Immediately go back to the next question on your script

We don't want to pay a real estate commission.

This one is great! Guess what, I don't like to put gas in my car, but I don't want to walk. I also don't like paying a doctor, but I do know that when I have a health problem, I want to get well as soon as possible.

We need to focus on what they do want. They want to sell their house. Overcome this objection quickly and get back to your script.

Here is how I would handle this objection.

> Seller: We are not ready to list our house.

> Agent: no problem, you do want to sell your house, correct? (let them answer)

> Immediately go back to the next question on your script

We will Pay You 3% if you bring a buyer

This is my favorite objection for these reasons

1. They are offering to pay me. Maybe it isn't what I charge, but they see value in my service.
2. These sellers are open to the possibility of working with me
3. They are super easy to set an appointment with

When you get this objection, you should get excited! At this point, you are just justifying your value and negotiating your commissions. I never negotiate commissions over the phone. Set an appointment as quickly as possible, ask for their email address and send your pre-listing package.

Seller: We will pay you 3% if you bring a buyer.

Agent: Fantastic: Will you be home at 4pm today?

Seller: (yes)

Agent: great I am going to stop by and take a look at your home so that we can see if we have a buyer for you. What is your email address? I want to send you some information on me and my team, so you know who is coming by? (send your pre-listing package asap).

We want to do some updates before we put our house on the market

I love this objection. I get to truly offer some guidance and really help my clients.

Depending on the neighborhood, market and price range, many upgrades are nice, but provide no real additional dollar value when it comes to selling.

I have had sellers in the past over-improve a home thinking they will get more money, but learn that those upgrades were only important to them or they have appraisal issues.

I also have had sellers in the past remodel a home and just make bad choices. For example, painting the home bold colors that go with their personal decor and taste rather than colors that would really work for a wide range of buyers and compliment the home.

I would try to get face to face with the sellers as quickly as possible to assist them in this process.

Here is the script:

> Seller: We want to do some updates before we put our house on the market

Agent: Fantastic, I'll tell you what, how about I come over and take a look? I have a lot of clients that do work before putting their home on the market.

I can help you make some choices that will save you some money and help make sure you get a return on the money you are investing in these upgrades.

(set an appointment, make sure to send your pre-listing package)

We already have an agent

This is a common objection. I always feel like, if it isn't on MLS and they are attempting to do it FSBO, they more than likely do not have paperwork signed and probably do not have an agent.

I have had some cases where I would ask "who is the agent?" and they would give me a name that wasn't in MLS or someone who wasn't even in the business any longer.

This is an objection to get you off the phone, most agents never inquire any further.

Here is how I handle this objection.

>Seller: We already have an agent.

>Agent: Fantastic, Who is your agent?

>Seller: (let them answer, they might not even have an agent)

>Agent: I tell you what, how about I send you over our marketing plan? You can look over it and compare it to theirs? There might be a few things you can steal from it, (haha) this plan sold (number of homes your office sold last year) homes last year. What is your email?

(follow up)

Often times I will follow up to make sure they received my email. Normally if they have talked to another agent, that agent does not have any written marketing plan.

Call us Back after the Holidays

This objection is popular among sellers around Christmas and Thanksgiving.

Here is how I would handle this objection

Seller: Call us back after the holidays.

Agent: Mr/Mrs seller. Let me ask you a quick question before I let you go. Do you all really need to sell your home? (yes) The reason I ask is this time of year we do not have as many buyers looking as we do in the spring and summer, but the ones that are looking are very serious. Plus inventory is a lot lower in the winter months.

(Make a weekly follow up plan for this lead. If you wait until after the holidays a lot more agents are going to be calling. You do not want them to forget you)

Where were you when our home was listed before? (expired)

Most expired sellers don't understand there are thousands of homes on our local MLS and typically their agent didn't do anything to make their home stand out. Sometimes they just had bad pictures, a bad description and never answered their phone. Sometimes its just the home didn't sell, it was priced well, just bad timing.

This is the script I would use.

Mr/Mrs seller
That is a great question. I look on MLS dailey at all of the homes on the market. Plus I talk to a lot of agents. Your previous agent, didn't let me know about your home.

I am looking at it right now online. Do you still want to sell it?

I can tell you exactly why it didn't sell. (let them answer)

(set appointment)

If you are looking for a full expired plan to add to your

business, you can find my book "How to be an Expired Master" on Amazon.

You are the (insert number) agent to call me today!!! (expired)

Typically, these sellers have not had near as many calls as they claim. When you go from getting 2 calls a day to getting 10 in the same day it just feels like a lot.

We really need to focus our call on "selling" their house, not "listing" their house.

> Seller: You are the 30th agent to call me today!!

> Agent: Wow that is a lot!! Have you really had 30 call?

> Seller: Yes

> Agent: They all were asking you to let them list your house? (let them answer)

> Seller: Yes

> Agent: I am not calling you to talk about listing your house. (oh)

> I am calling you about selling your house, are you still interested in selling your house?

(continue with your original script)

If you are looking for a full expired plan to add to your business, you can find my book "How to be an Expired Master" on Amazon.

We want to hire an agent with an office closer to our house.

This is one of those cases where the seller just does not really understand how real estate agents work and how our local MLS system works.

In today's market, location of your office really does not matter a whole lot as far as success in an area. In my market, I have primarily lived on the very southern end of our MLS coverage area but most of the business I have pursued was on the very north end of west side of our market and has been 30 minutes or more away from the location I actually had an office in .

Here is the script I would use to handle this objection.

> Seller: We want to hire an agent with an office closer to our property

> Agent: Mr/Mrs Seller. I understand what you are saying.

> I sell a lot of houses, if you are not really interested in selling your house I can't spend much time working on it.

> Let me ask you, do you really want to sell your house or are you just testing the market? (yes we want to sell it)

Fantastic, our office has sold (x) houses within (distance) of yours.

Can we meet this afternoon, so I can see your home?

We can sell our house on our own

Usually these sellers believe they can sell their home on their own. A lot of them are trying to save money or think they can actually get more. In reality, it is hard to sell your house on your own in a normal market.

In this case, I would get as much information as possible and attempt to meet them face to face.

Seller: We can sell our house on our own

Agent: Mr/Mrs Seller. That is great. You do want to sell your house, correct? (yes) So you have sold your own home before?

(seller: yes)

Fantastic, let me ask you, we specialize in working with homes in your price range. If I could get you enough so that you could walk away with $_____ would you be interested?

(if they say no)

This is a great lead, follow up regularly and you are waiting until they decide they need help.

(if they say yes)

(set an appointment ASAP)

For more information or to join my group coaching you can go to
http://www.JasonMorrisGroupCoaching.com 45

We are just testing the market

They could be telling the truth, but usually there is a lot of thought and discussion before making a decision that would end in, packing all of your stuff up and moving your entire life. I rarely believe this objection.

I would plan to follow up with this lead.

However , this is how I would handle the first call.

Seller: We are just testing the market

Agent: Fantastic, what are you testing it for? (let them answer)

Oh, what happens if a buyer pops up and offers you the (asking price) you are advertising?

We are taking it off the market for a little while

Usually this is a situation where whatever problem they had that made them consider selling their home has passed, gotten worked out or they have just settled into it.

This is a great lead to put into a follow up plan.

> Here is how I would handle this lead.
>
> Seller: We are taking it off the market for a little while.
>
> Agent: I understand, it's hard having to have your house ready all the time for showings.
>
> If I had a buyer that would give you the (asking price) you were looking for? Would you all be interested?
>
> (if they say no)
>
> I always like to know what homes are coming up for sale, when do you think you might try again? (let them answer)
>
> (follow up)

**** If they say yes****
Go back to your original script and set an appointment.

If you are looking for a full expired plan to add to your business, you can find my book "How to be an Expired Master" on Amazon.

We are looking for someone with more experience

This is an object I often hear new agents in my coaching group get. You can always partner up with a more experienced agent in your office to co-list it.

Here is how I would handle this objection.

> Seller: We are looking for someone with more experience
>
> Agent: Mr/Mrs Seller. I understand I do not have as much experience as a lot of agents. However, I am aggressive and I would not be working on selling your home by myself. My team I work with has over ___ years experience and sold over ___ homes last year.
>
> I am not sure you can find someone with that sort of support. You did look at my marketing plan I sent over? That plan has sold (firm's history #) homes. If it has worked for that many sellers I know it is going to work for you too.

I want to talk to my Spouse before setting an appointment

This objection may be true. Maybe they want to make sure there are not any time conflicts. I suggest "penciling in" an appointment with them. They can always call back and re-schedule or cancel.

Here is how I would respond.

> Seller: I want to talk to my spouse before setting an appointment
>
> Agent: No problem. I encourage you to talk to them, I would like to meet you both. Do they normally work during the day? (yes or no)
>
> How about this, my schedule fills up quick, what if I pencil you in for (date/time) if that doesn't work for them you can call me back and we can figure out a time that will?

I am willing to pay x% commission

Typically this is a lessor commission than what we normally charge but, it is a good sign. I like to look at it as they are willing to work with me, we are just negotiating what I will be charging.

Here is how I would handle this objection. I would set an appointment As soon as possible.

The idea to lower your commission is a business decision.

Ask yourself where is the best place for a sign?

In the trunk of your car or someone's front yard?

We interviewed an agent that offered a lower commission

This is an objection that normally you would only get it on the phone after the appointment or while you are sitting at their kitchen table going through your presentation with the seller.

Here is how I would handle this commission objection.

> Seller: we interviewed an agent that offered a lower commission
>
> Agent: There are agents that do charge more than we do and some that charge less. Did you compare their marketing plan to the one of mine I sent you?
>
> (answer)
>
> What commission rate did they offer? (let them answer)
>
> (make a business decision)

We couldn't sell our home in time, so we decided to rent it out

This is very common when the market starts to change and slow down.

This lead would be on my long term monthly follow up list. Eventually the tenant will move out. During the time it is rented you can build a relationship and hopefully be first in line when the home goes empty again.

Here is the script I would use.

> Seller: We had to rent our house out.

> Agent: I understand. We often sell rented homes to investors and people who are ready to buy but not ready to move yet. We often can work around your tenants.

> Typically if a seller is very desperate, they probably rented to the first tenant that came along, with very little screening. With this lead you know 2 things, the lease is probably for a year and the seller was desperate. I would recommend following up once a month with market statistics and information of value.

You can get your full 1 year seller follow up strategy from www.FollowupMasterDayPlanner.com

We are having a lot of interest right now by ourselves. (FSBO)

The initial excitement of putting your home on craigslist is always great. The average seller doesn't have the experience or the time to deal with the calls and the questions they often get.

Here is the script I would use.

Seller: We are getting a lot of calls from craigslist.

Agent: Fantastic, I know you have your home on (website). The great thing about that website is it is free, the bad thing I have is everyone is looking to rent or looking for owner financing. (pause and let them respond)

What kind of time frame do you need to sell in? (answer)
Oh.... (sound sad) you know it typically takes a home about 60 days to close and that is if you had a contract today.

Let me help you. I'll tell you what I can do. I can come out and give you my opinion and start working for you. You guys keep doing what you are doing. If you find a buyer first we can cancel our contract.

(Making this sort of promise or deal over the last 15 years, I have only had 2 times a seller found a buyer on their own)

If you are looking for a full FSBO system you can find my book "How to be a FSBO Master" on Amazon.

We want to use a company with a bigger name

This happens every now and then. Typically if you use a pre-listing package and have a good sales process you can easily overcome this objection.

Here is how I would handle it.

> Seller: We want to use a company with a bigger name.
>
> Agent: Wow… So your home can be just another number?
> (let them answer)
> I guarantee we are going to do a lot more for you than the big name companies. Typically those companies have a big name because they are spending all of their money marketing their name, not your house.
>
> Let me send you over my marketing plan that tells what we do to sell houses. What is your email?

We want to sell to a Cash Investor

Every now and then, I will hear this objection. The problem is, the investors with real cash are typically looking for real deals. Most sellers, unless they are truly super motivated, are not willing to take the offer many cash investors are willing to pay.

Here is the script I would use.

> Seller: We want to sell to a cash investor.
>
> Agent: I understand, what was your asking price again? (answer) That looks to be pretty close to market value. I often have cash buyers. How much are you willing to discount it?
>
> Seller: (none)
>
> Wow, what most of these guys are doing is looking for super motivated people, so they can buy at a discount, paint, put down new carpet and resell for a profit.
>
> Could you wait 60 to 90 day, If I could get you (asking price)?
>
> (If yes, set an appointment. If no, follow up in a week)

For more information or to join my group coaching you can go to
http://www.JasonMorrisGroupCoaching.com 59

We don't want to sell any more

Sometimes this happens. If they don't want to sell, you can't really do much to make them.

I always ask:

> Why not?
>
> If I brought you a cash offer for (asking price) you wouldn't be interested?
>
> It never hurts to follow up with these sellers.

We just aren't ready right now

Sometimes this is the case. Maybe they are waiting to hear back from a job or waiting for the school year to end. Sometimes they are just trying to figure out where would they go if they sold their home. It usually isn't as complicated as what we try to make it.

Seller: We just are not ready right now.

> Agent: No problem, what needs to happen before you are ready to sell your home?
>
> Do you have a time frame?
>
> (Follow up)

You can find my full 1 year plan for follow up at www.FollowupMasterDayPlanner.com

I don't have a price, someone will just make me an offer

This usually is not how it works. When I have gotten this objection, a lot of times I would go ahead and do just a quick market analysis on MLS and asking "what about somewhere between ($xxx,xxx and $xxx,xxx), would that work?

Everyone has a number they are willing to sell for.

Generally these people giving this objection are delusional. However, it never hurts to follow up and whatever has drove them to put up a FSBO ad may motivate them to actually want to take action in the future.

I have already interviewed agents.

If they have interviewed multiple agents, they probably all were about the same. However, they usually have not picked an agent because they didn't find one that had a plan they really believed in.

Here is the script I would use.

> Seller: We have already interviewed agents.
>
> Agent: No kidding. Did you find one you liked? I bet they all promised you the world right? (haha)
>
> (yes, no)
>
> I understand, let me send you over my marketing plan. It is in writing and its probably different that anything you have gotten. Worse case you can steal some of our strategies that sold (X number) houses last year. What is your email?

I can't meet you, I don't live in the area

This is so common in second home markets. A lot of agents do not know how to handle these sorts of leads. This is a script that has been very successful for me in the past.

> Seller: I can't meet you, I don't live in the area
>
> Agent: No Problem. How about this? I am going to be out in the (area) today. How about I drive by the home and take a quick look at the outside and give you a call back? Would it be ok if I walked around the house?
>
> Call back while you are at the house!! Do not forget to call while you are standing on the property.

Have you sold any homes in the area?

I don't think it is an objection as much as a question. However, I understand with newer agents if you haven't sold anything in the area it can be challenging. If this is the case, I would constantly look to the experience and track record of my office.

Here is how I would handle this question.

Seller: Have you sold any homes in the area?

Agent: Yes, Our team aggressively works in your area. I would like to send you over our plan that shows what we do to sell homes. What is your email?

(get their email)

Will you be home tomorrow around 4pm? I will be in your area, I would like to stop by.

We are going to re-list with our previous agent

With expired listings it seems about ⅓ of the sellers will probably re-list with the previous agent. This may be different in your market, but it is a common objection we have in mine.

This is how I would handle this objection.

> Seller: We are going to re-list with our previous agent.
>
> Agent: Oh wow. Didn't they have it listed for (6 months)?
>
> Seller: yes they did
>
> Agent: Let me ask you a quick question, are you all serious about selling your home? Or are you guys just testing the market?
>
> Seller: (we are serious)
>
> Agent: Mr/Mrs seller. I want to send you over our marketing plan on what we do to sell homes. I can tell you exactly why your home hasn't sold.
>
> I will be in your area this afternoon. How about I stop by, it will take me about 15 minutes, I will

not waste your time..

If you are looking for a full expired plan, you can find my book "How to be an Expired Master on Amazon".

I checked out zillow….

We all know Zillow/Trulia/Realtor(dot)com have inaccuracies. I have tried to avoid talking about these large national websites and steer the conversation to data and information that I personally know is true and accurate.

> Address their question or statement and move forward.
>
> Here is how I would handle this sort of objection or question.
>
> Seller: I checked out Zillow and _____.
>
> Agent: Oh yes? Zillow is having a lot of inaccuracies lately. I really hope they get it straight.
>
> Mr/Mrs Seller, did you look at the marketing plan I sent you?

We are going to wait and see if the market comes up some.

These people are trying to time the market. Just as the market goes up, it can easily go down. Usually in this case, they are upside down or they need a certain dollar amount in order to move on to their next home.

Here is how I handle this objection.

> Seller: We are going to wait and see if the market goes up some.

> Agent: I understand, do you have a price point you need to get?

> (get as much information and follow up)

We want to wait until the Spring.

The best thing to do with this objection is to ask more questions.

Here is how I would handle it.

> Seller: We want to wait until the Spring.
>
> Agent: I understand, a lot of sellers want to wait until the Spring. Usually inventory goes up like crazy in the spring.
>
> Mr/Mrs seller, if we could get your price, would you be willing to sell your home now? Or is something happening in the spring that you need to wait for?
>
> (follow up)

I am taken care of (then hangs up)

When this happens, think about how you handle telemarketers. This is the same thing that happened to you. They are not taken care of, its just not a good time right now.

> I would plan to follow up with this lead in a couple of days or even in the late afternoon.

I would like my attorney to look over the paperwork

Unbelievably, I have been on listing appointments with other agents and they really had no idea what the paperwork said. Some of them couldn't even fill in the blanks correctly on the contract.

I think one of the most important things you can do is learn how to effectively go through the common forms your office uses and learn to properly explain them to someone else. Do not read them the 11 page document, actually explain it to them.

If you are getting this objection over and over, you need to plan some time to work on going over this paperwork. Actually read each paragraph, write yourself out a script paraphrasing each section and practice it.

Here is how I would handle this objection.

> Seller: I would like my attorney to look over the paperwork.
>
> Agent: No problem. This is a standard agreement that the real estate association provides. How about if I go over it real quick with you. Maybe I can answer your questions and save you some attorney fees?

What are you going to do different than all of the other agents calling me?

This is a very good question. Have your pre-listing package ready!

Here is how I would handle this question.

> Seller: What are you going to do different that all of the other agents calling me?
>
> Agent: Haha....well I actually sell houses. If I didn't think I could sell your, I wouldn't call you. You do want to sell your house right?
>
> Seller: Yes we do
>
> Agent: Let me send you over some information about me, my team and our marketing plan that sells houses.

I want to meet with 1 more agent. (after you)

This statement really makes me feel like they are serious about working with a real estate agent. They are just getting a second opinion. No problem. I am going to make sure they have my pre-listing package and I am going to ask them to compare our marketing plans. I know that most agents do not have a written marketing plan.

Here is how I would handle this

> Seller: I want to meet with 1 more agent.
>
> Agent: No problem. There is one thing I want to ask you to do? (ok) You have my marketing package, go ahead and request theirs so you can put them side by side and compare.
>
> Now you need to follow up the next day.

We are meeting an agent (before you)

This statement really makes me feel like they are serious about working with a real estate agent. In this objection you are the second opinion. No problem. Just like the previous objection, I am going to make sure they have my pre-listing package and I am going to ask them to compare our marketing plans. I know that most agents do not have a written marketing plan. This time I really want to get my marketing plan to them before they meet the other agent.

Here is how I would handle this

> Seller: I want to meet with 1 more agent.

> Agent: No problem. There is one thing I want to ask you to do? (ok) You have my marketing package, go ahead and request theirs so you can put them side by side and compare.

> Now you need to follow up to make sure they received your email and also make sure they got the other agents…. Or didn't get the other agents.

Conclusion

I hope this book has given you a lot of insight on objections and ideas on how you can handle common objections you are getting when you are calling home seller leads.

I also included some basic scripts for you.

FSBO Script

Hey Mr. Seller, This is (your name) with (Realty Company), I'm calling about your house. Is it still for sale?

What will you take for it? (Let him answer)
How soon do you want to sell it?

Ask questions about stuff in the ad if you are calling from the ad (during this time pull comps)

Ask other questions Questions such as:

Is your home in good shape?
How old is the roof?
How old is the HVAC?

Once you get an idea of comps say

I can get you enough so that you can put $(seller price) in your pocket after my fees and attorney fees are paid. Would you be ok with that?

Will you be available at 4 pm tomorrow? (Or any time that fits your schedule)

Great!

I like to send over a package that tells a little bit about my team and me and what we do
to sell homes. What is your email address? (9 out of 10 give it to me with no hesitation)
I'll send it to you in a few minutes. (Send it to them ASAP! Then text to ensure they
received it)

Ok. I will plan to see you tomorrow at 4 pm? (You set the time)
Remember you are only calling to get a price, gauge motivation and set an
appointment. You can ask him questions about moving etc. when you get there if you
want to. On the phone only ask questions about his home and what time you can see it.

Your goal is to set an appointment.
End of Script

Expired Script

Hey Mr. Seller, This is (your name) with (Realty Company). Do you still want to sell your house at (Address)? (yes)

How much will you take for it? (let them answer)

I saw you had it on the market, why do you think it didn't it sell? (let them answer)

I have been doing some research, I believe I know why your old agent didn't sell it. How soon do you want to get rid of this place? (let them answer)

Confirm information you see in MLS - example

So this home is a 3 bedroom 2 bath with a garage?
It has a new roof?
It is on a half of an acre?

Fantastic!

Will you be home this afternoon (or tomorrow, you state the time always)? (yes)
I am going to be in your area, can I stop by at 4pm?

(ok) (try to set an appointment
asap, other agents are calling)

I want to send you some information about me, so
you know who will be stopping by
your house? What is your email address? (send
them your pre-listing package asap)
Confirm Your appointment and show up early!!

www.ingramcontent.com/pod-product-compliance
Lightning Source LLC
Chambersburg PA
CBHW020607220526
45463CB00006B/2489